OVERHEARD
ON THE ISLAND

THE FUNNY, FOOLISH, AND
FANTASTIC THINGS ISLANDERS
COME OUT WITH

David Weale
Charlottetown
2003

Overheard on the Island:
The Funny, Foolish, and Fantastic Things Islanders Come Out With
David Weale, 2003
Other titles by David Weale include:
    Them Times
    An Island Christmas Reader
    A Long Way from the Road
And for children:
    The True Meaning of Crumbfest
    Everything That Shines

Cover Design by Chloe Cork

Printed and bound in Canada by Transcontential, Borden-Carleton, PE

National Library of Canada Cataloguing in Publication Data
Weale, David, 1942-
    Overheard On The Island : The Funny, Foolish and Fantastic
Things Islanders Come Out With

ISBN 0-9733792-0-0
1. Prince Edward Islanders –Quotations. 2. Prince Edward Island–
Quotations, maxims, etc. 3. Canadianism (English)–Prince Edward
Island. 4. Prince Edward Island–Humor. 5. Canadian wit and humor
(English)–Prince Edward Island. I. Title.

FC2611.3W42 2003   971.7'04'0207
C2003-905159-5

Published by
Tangle Lane Productions
195 North River Road
Charlottetown, PE
C1A 3L4

Acknowledgements

Thanks, first of all, to the hundreds of Islanders who made this volume possible just by talking. They spoke it into existence and I'm grateful for every word.

My thanks also to Gary MacDougall, managing editor at *The Guardian*, for making available a daily corner in the newspaper for this collection of sayings. I can't say how often I have been told by Islanders that they enjoy the "Overheard" quotes, and that they turn to them everyday. One woman delivered the ultimate compliment. She confessed that sometimes she reads the "little sayings" even before she turns to the death notices, and then added, "Isn't that awful." And I knew immediately I had another quote.

Introduction

The everyday talk of Islanders often amuses me greatly, and occasionally stirs me deeply. Sometimes it's an unexpected choice of words that grabs my attention, or an alerting tone of voice, or the curious cut of some local accent, or the burst of energy with which the words are delivered. In other instances it's the eccentricity of the Island point of view I find so compelling, and in still others the acidic quality common to both Island soil and Island speech. And sometimes, when I'm fortunate, it's all of the above, combined in a single sentence or phrase. When that happens I stop whatever I'm doing and begin looking for a pen and a piece of paper. I've been doing that for years, and it's where this collection of quotations originated. It's a record of all those instances when my fellow Islanders stopped me in my tracks by saying something so comical, or pithy, or outrageous, that I felt the need to record it.

Not all the sayings were collected from the original sources. On the Island quotes and rumours - like cousins - are usually once or twice removed from the direct line. Islanders savour, and enjoy recycling, the witticisms of friends and acquaintances, and they are not above doctoring the information to make the retelling even more interesting. That's how many of these quotes came to me - from those who had heard them from those who had heard them from someone else. It means, doubtless, that in many instances the original utterances have been modified. Words have been changed along the way, and I confess to altering a few myself, but in every instance I believe the wit and intent of the originator shines through.

  Collecting these sayings was a pleasant task, for it appealed to the powerful gathering instinct I seem to have inherited from my foraging forebears. I enjoy picking blueberries; I enjoy digging clams; and I have enjoyed gathering these *bons mots* of oral currency. Fortunately, many Islanders possess a gift for aphorism and simile, which is a legacy of the strong oral culture that existed here until recent years. Further, I believe that because of our insularity, our strong communalism, and the delicacy of many of our relationships we have a natural inclination toward cryptic humour and finely distilled understatement. We are an ironic, not a brash people, for we have learned that when you say too much there is no corner where you can hide; or, as one woman expressed it, "I don't think it's very polite to get right to the point." The result of this caution is a talent for indirectness that is almost universal; a talent frequently expressed in clever one-liners.

A few of the sayings in the book are my own, but most are from the lips of others. I know this makes some Islanders nervous being around me, and occasionally someone will tell me something really good and then add, "And don't you dare put that in the paper." But I'm often not sure whether they mean it, or whether it's a camouflaged way of reminding me they've just said something worth quoting. So if I meet you on the street, or at some gathering, and you say something especially funny or wise, with an Island flavour, you perhaps might worry that I will remember what you said, and copy it down at the first opportunity. Well...

"My mother said I
should go to the
wake because the
dead man's brother
used to pick up the
cream cans at her
uncle's farm."

"When I was a kid it cost $25.00 to go around the world, and I didn't have enough money to get out of sight."

"Were you born on
the Island, or did
you come here on
purpose?"

"Tell me this will ya,
do we have the worst
goddamned drivers in
the world, or do I
just need a
tranquilizer?"

"I don't know if he's an alcoholic, but he can't go to the mailbox without a case of beer."

"I met a lot of
famous people
workin' on the boat.
A lot of
wrestlers...and
Tommy Hunter."

1st person:"Are
George and Alfred
still workin'?"
2nd person:"Oh ya.
They've had an awful
siege of it this year."

"The visitors in the summer didn't used to be total strangers."

"I remember right well the time a bunch of us walked all the way to French River to see an electric fence."

"We didn't use the word 'gay' back then. If a man was like that we called him a 'fluffy fella'".

"Any man who would
vote different than
his own father is not
a man at all."

"It used to be the custom to hold your breath when you drove across the railway tracks, or across a bridge... (pause) I guess that's not such a good idea anymore."

"In Egmont Bay games between the Montreal Canadiens and the Toronto Maple Leafs were like a holy war. People would say their beads on behalf of the Canadiens."

"It's hard to come right out and speak your mind on the Island. It's why the soil is red - from the biting of so many tongues."

"He got interested in his ancestors, but when he asked his father where they came from he replied, 'We were from King Street originally.'"

"All the fishermen
believed that you
don't ever turn your
boat against the sun,
because it was bad
luck. You'd turn it
with the sun."

"Charles," he said, "I see your field is not long enough for your furrows."

"I missed home more than I expected, and every night when the sun went down I envied it, because I knew it was headed for the Island."

"They were difficult to entertain. Like burning wet wood."

"All their kids were slow; too stupid to box strawberries."

"He's not an altogether bad fella, but meetin' up with him is like a feed of smelts - once a year is enough."

"My father was a
fisherman, and when
it was time for bed
he would always say,
'Time for blanket
harbour.'"

"People generally were careful not to marry too close, you know what I mean. But there was a lot of mental inbreeding."

"Eat? You never seen the like. You had to feed him spruce boughs first to put a bottom in him."

"He's as useless as a fiddler's fart."

"I am the baby of fifteen children, so I was an aunt before I was even born."

"When they were in Edmonton they talked about the Island like it was heaven, but I knew as soon as they came home they'd be grumbling about everything."

"The minute I went
into labour he was
gone like a bat out of
hell, out to the barn
with the horse. I
don't think I seen
him for two days."

34

"He can't keep his wife in paint and powder, let alone pills."

"The Island is hell
for jealousy. They'll
do anything to help
you up, and anything
to pull you down if ya
get up too far."

"He told me when he was my age he had to hook it under the fence to save his eyes, but that now he has to lay it over the fence to save his boots."

"When he didn't want
to tell us where he
was going he'd say,
'I'm off to the
Magdalen Islands for
a load of postholes.'"

"In sickness and in health wasn't just about marriage. It was that way between neighbours too."

1st person:"You should do a little travelling, and meet new people."
2nd person:"What's the point of that? I've met all the people I can stand right now."

"None of the boys in that family turned out any good, and I don't know what the problem was - their father certainly beat them enough."

"I was so shy and backward I went with a girl for six years and she didn't even know it."

"The rum that came off those vessels during prohibition was that strong it would split your tongue."

"There's Islanders, and then there's up-west Islanders, and that's another thing altogether."

"If old Mary didn't have Alzheimer's I'd get you to call her right now. Christ, that woman had more remedies than you can count. Had one for everything."
(Pause)
"Except Alzheimer's I guess."

"They called it the ferry 'terminal' because sometimes that's exactly how it felt."

"Many people try to hide the fact that they're poor, but on the Island there's also a lot of people trying to hide the fact that they're rich."

"They bragged him up so high I thought they had the wrong man in the casket. And he owed three people money that I knew of."

"He's a proud devil,
and hard to help.
Like an injured
skunk."

"The Doctor told me
I had to give up sex,
but I didn't know
whether he meant
thinking about it or
talking about it."

"The old people, oh
my God Almighty,
they would scare the
shit right out of you
with them ghost
stories."

"My Uncle Jim loves
those quotes of
yours in the paper,
and he's not even
from here."

"If it's a lie from me
it was a lie to me."

"I dread meeting up
with him. He comes
on like bad weather."

"Did you ever notice that the Island is shaped like a boomerang, and that everything you say comes back to you?"

1st Man: "What would
you buy if you won
the lottery?"
(Pause)
2nd Man: "A new chain
saw."

"I'm not saying he's slow, but he'd be a good one to send for death."

1st Person:
"Great day!"
2nd Person:
"Near time!"

"I'm glad I lived this long because there are a lot of people I couldn't stand who are gone."

"He fell out of the stupid tree and hit every branch on the way down."

"Don't put your winter duds away until the leaves are right out on the trees. And there'll be a couple of days after that you'll wish you had them."

"I lived in the dirt. I slept in the dirt, and I ate the dirt, and when I came home I kissed the dirt."

Returned W.W.II Veteran

Minister: "Let us now pray for the rain we so desperately need." Parishioner to the man next to him: "What's the use of praying for rain when the wind is out of the west?"

"After our wedding breakfast [in Morell] we went into Charlottetown for dinner, and then out to the airport to watch the planes."

64

"It comes from being
Scotch. You could
be influenced by
someone, but you
don't really give in.
We were very hard
people to tell
something to that
might help us."

"Mona's husband was a terrible alcoholic for years and years, but she told me she never once actually saw him take a drink."

"I asked a young
fellow the other day
to pick some
raspberries. 'No,' he
said, 'there's too
many flies.'
(pause)
The good-for-
nothing young
bugger."

"You didn't look for a divorce, you just disappeared."

"It was an uphill job
all the way. I
farmed for over
fifty years and never
caught up."

"He used to keep the volume on the radio turned way down as a way of saving money."

"She explained matter-of-factly to the other woman that I wasn't an Islander, but that I had lived here all my life."

"She looked so good
I went to the wake
twice, just to be
sure it was her."

"I had never been to
Prince Edward Island
in my life, but
everybody kept
asking me, 'When did
you get home?'"

"This is an Island of secrets, but everybody knows them."

1st Man:"I'm half-Protestant."
2nd Man:"Which half?"
1st Man:"The half that can't have any fun."

"It's damn hard to
get ahead I'll tell you
that. There's always
something to keep
the rabbit's tail
short."

"He wasn't what
you'd call a big
success, but he could
have gone farther
and done worse."

"The burden of being an Islander is the burden of having to be friendly all the time."

"I wish they'd cut
down every
goddamned tree in
the woods so no one
would ever be able to
make another
fiddle."

"My father hated me
so much he left me
the farm."

"Mother had
arthritis, then
inward cancer. She
suffered a lot. She
was a great
sufferer."

"The day the car arrived at our farm in Valleyfield the neighbours all came over, and many gathered around the auto for photographs. Mother served a lunch."

"A mild winter like
this isn't healthy,
but it makes the
graves easy to dig."

"He's lied so
goddamned much he
has to get the
neighbour over to
call the dog."

Comment about a local politician

"All they care about
is how fast they can
get off the Island,
and how fast they
can get back. It's
rash thinking."

"I had too much
respect for my
husband ever to let
him see me naked."

"I wouldn't say we
were prejudiced.
We even had a
Catholic work for us.
He ate supper with
us and everything."

"In our area couples
living common-law
were given an
especially hard time
on Halloween."

"Why do you think
Islanders are so
interested in politics
anyway? It's
patronage boy,
patronage. It's what
makes us so
democratic."

"I like turnips but my sister-in-law can't touch them because they bring back so many sad memories."

"I don't know him,
but I know of him
through the wife's
brother."

"One day I read one
of those quotes of
yours in the paper
and I laughed so
hard I scared the
dog."

"My aunt came home
from Boston every
summer and she
would always say,
'Those draggers will
be the ruination of
the fishery.' She
could see it."

"As a kid growin' up
on the farm ya might
not have felt wanted,
but ya always felt
needed."

"It's a great summer
all right, but we'll
pay up for it this
winter."

"No I don't like the Bridge. Now you set off for somewhere on the other side and the first thing you know you're there. What kind of a God-blessed trip is that?"

"It is the God-given right of every Islander to know the business and the whereabouts of every other Islander."

"On PEI your funeral
is considered the
biggest event of
your life."

"The old man who
lived next to us had
never travelled, but
was quite sure there
was no place like the
Island."

"Crop rotation on
Island farms means
potatoes - then
snow."

"Oh the natives, the natives. I'm tired of hearin' about them. Do they think they're the only ones with problems?"

"I don't care what
you say, I still don't
think it's a good idea
to mix milk and
lobsters."

"Rhubarb would get
my vote for the
Island plant. It gets
through the winter
so well you know...
(pause)
and it's fairly sour."

"My husband could be awful sarcastic. If the vegetables weren't cooked enough he'd say, 'You gave them an awful scaldin'.'"

"One Sunday afternoon we drove up to Borden to go across on the new ferry; but when we got over there we decided there was probably nothing to see, so we just stayed on the boat."

"We met a car driving
with its lights on
during the day and
grandfather said
they must have a lot
of money to be able
to do that."

"When I was little I use to thank God for three things: that my father didn't drink, that there were no bears left on the Island; and that our family was Conservative."

"The way we're farming today is like stealing from the future."

"When we'd be
heading for the ferry
mother would get out
the beads in the car
and say the Rosary,
so we would have a
safe journey and
catch the boat."

1st Woman leaving wake: "My, but didn't he look good?"
2nd Woman: "Why wouldn't he look good? He spent half the winter in Florida."